"Cross Stitch" Quilts

Eleanor Burns

a Quilt in a Day® publication

Roses for Teresa! Thank you for all your help.

First printing October, 2000

Published by Quilt in a Day®, Inc.
1955 Diamond St, San Marcos, CA 92069

©2000 by Eleanor A. Burns Family Trust

ISBN 1-891776-04-5

Art Director Merritt Voigtlander

Table of Contents

Introduction

For many years, our crochet and cross stitch patterns were influenced by the work of Anne Champe Orr. A Nashville, Tennessee native, Anne lived from 1875 to 1946. I first "met" Anne through her photograph as a judge for the Sears Century of Progress quilt contest in 1933. She looked very regal in a little black hat and black dress with high neck band.

Readers of *Good Housekeeping Magazine* were familiar with her work through her Art needlework column from 1919 to 1940. During that time, Anne also worked for JP Coats and Clark Thread and loved to feature instructions on crochet, especially those with a pictorial design. When quilts became popular in the 1930's, she designed quilts influenced from cross stitch. To achieve the cross stitch appearance, she made the patterns from 1" finished size squares.

The antique Heirloom Basket quilt (right) was one of four cross stitch type designs featured in January 1935 issue of *Good Housekeeping Magazine*. Her favorite motif was a basket with bow, and flowers. This one is a beauty in delicate pastels and shading in solid colors.

The second antique quilt is French Wreath, typical of an Anne Orr design with the center wreath medallion. The 1⅛" green strips separate the pillow and side sections. It's also made of dainty 1" squares. I referenced this pattern in the Mountain Mist catalogue, probably influenced by Anne Orr.

I was ecstatic to find an original copy of one of Anne's booklets, *Filet Crochet Second book, Cross Stitch Designs*, originally sold for 25 cents!

French Wreath Antique Quilt, Maker Unknown

Heirloom Basket Antique Quilt, Maker Unknown

At Anne's own admission, she knew little about the needle! Yet she was considered a highly successful businesswoman, and pioneer in quiltmaking. We can admire her work today, and be totally amazed by the patterns created by those tiny squares. I know Anne Orr would be impressed with the innovative way we can recreate her charming cross stitch designs.

Read more about the life of Anne Orr in *Soft Covers for Hard Times,* by Merikay Waldvogel, Rutledge Hill Press, 1990.

Eleanor Burns

Included in this booklet are crochet samples for borders, as well as patterns for cross stitch. Since color gradation was so important to the Orr Studio, Anne offered a full colored center fold of pattern suggestions.

Selecting a Design

Designs for these seven wallhangings and two queen size quilts are similar to Anne Orr's original drawings. However, the technique for creating them is entirely innovative! We created the "cross stitch" designs by simply arranging 1½" fabric squares on a 1½" grid of fusible interfacing, fusing the squares in place, and then sewing them together. Yardage, cutting charts, and finishing are included for wallhangings and quilts.

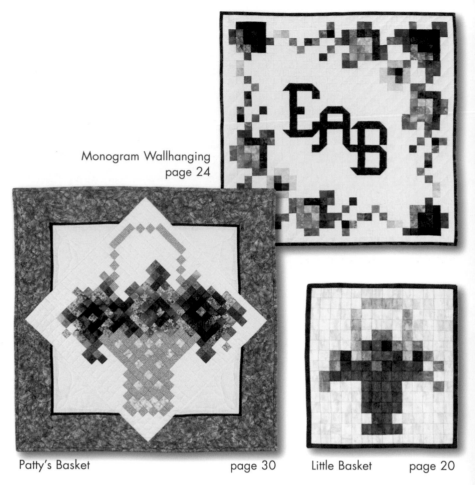

Monogram Wallhanging
page 24

Patty's Basket   page 30

Little Basket   page 20

Teresa's Basket   page 34

Pages from Anne Orr's original booklet

Victorian Basket with Border   page 28

Amber's Basket   page 18

Floral Wreath Quilt   page 38

Victorian Basket
page 26

Nosegay
page 22

Fusible Interfacing and Fabrics

Non-woven Fusible Interfacing

Projects in this book were made using a non-woven fusible interfacing printed with a 1½" grid. Fabric squares finish at 1". The grid is printed on the smooth side of the interfacing, and the fusing agent is on the opposite textured side. This product is available from several manufacturers.

HTC Inc. manufactures a 1½" fusible grid under the name Quilt Fuse™ in 48" width, with (32) 1½" squares across, and sold by the yard. Each project lists the number of squares needed.

QuiltSMART® manufactures a 1½" grid printed on a fusible panel 22½" wide. One panel is 15 squares across and 16 squares down. In the process of silk screening, a space is left on the interfacing between panels. This space can be used if the space is an accurate 1½". Each project lists the number of QuiltSMART® panels needed.

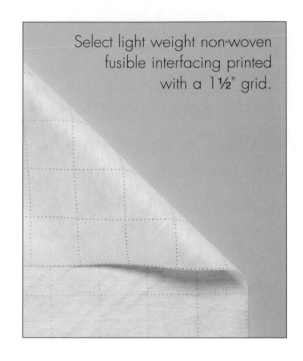

Select light weight non-woven fusible interfacing printed with a 1½" grid.

Plain Interfacing

If you can not find non-woven fusible interfacing printed with a 1½" grid, buy plain interfacing by the yard and mark your own grid. Each project lists how much yardage to purchase based on a 22½" width.

Place the plain interfacing on a cutting mat, fusible side up, and use the mat's lines as a guide for placing fabric squares. If you can't see the lines on the mat, draw a 1½" grid on the smooth side with a fine point permanent marking pen and 6" x 24" ruler.

Converting Projects

Printed fusible interfacing is available in sizes other than a 1½" grid. Although yardage is not included, you could create larger or smaller projects, just by changing the size of the grid.

HTC, Inc. has Quilt Fuse™ printed in a 2" grid at 48" wide, with (23) 2" squares across, and sold by the yard. Projects end up with 1½" finished squares as opposed to 1" finished squares. Use this product to enlarge the projects.

June Tailor has a 1" grid finishing at ½" printed on a 45" x 72" fusible sheet referred to as Quilt Top Express. This product is perfect for turning wallhangings into miniature quilts.

Fabrics

Select a Background fabric in a tone on tone in white, off-white, or pastel. The Background requires the most fabric, and in the finished quilt, offers an opportunity for extensive quilting.

Select three values of the same color to show shading and dimension in the flowers. Most quilts need pinks, yellows, blues, purples, golds, and greens. The multiple values, or gradation of one color should move gracefully from one to the next, without a drastic value change between each one. In most cases, ⅛ yard of each value is enough yardage per project. Many of the fabrics used were from the Color Reference Library by Benartex Fabrics, Inc.

Original Anne Orr quilts were made with solid colored fabrics. For a more interesting look, use **mottled hand dyed fabrics.** Robert Kaufman manufactures Kona® Multi Dye fabric that simulates the rich texture of hand-dyed fabric. One piece of mottled fabric with different values in the same piece will often give the variety needed.

An ombre fabric, or a fabric printed with texture in several values is also useful, particularly in the greens.

For added texture, select small flowers approximately ½" in size in monochromatic or analogous colors. Analogous colors are located side by side on the color wheel.

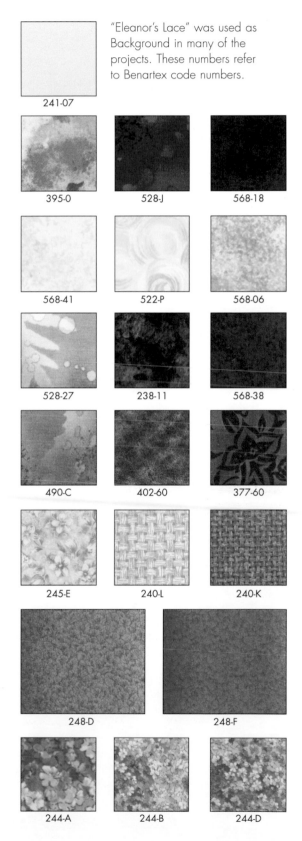

"Eleanor's Lace" was used as Background in many of the projects. These numbers refer to Benartex code numbers.

241-07

395-0   528-J   568-18

568-41   522-P   568-06

528-27   238-11   568-38

490-C   402-60   377-60

245-E   240-L   240-K

248-D   248-F

244-A   244-B   244-D

Supplies

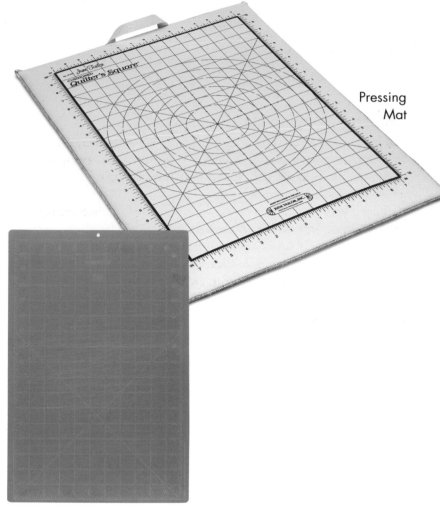

Pressing
Mat

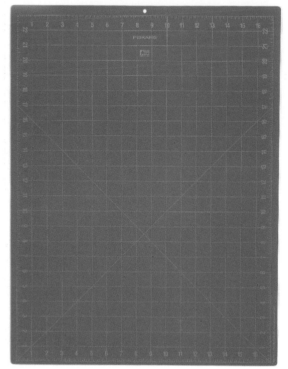

18" x 24" Cutting Mat

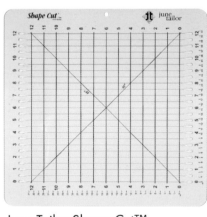

12" x 18" Cutting Mat

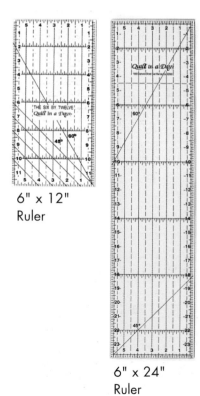

6" x 12"
Ruler

6" x 24"
Ruler

June Tailor Shape Cut™

Fine Point Permanent Marking Pen

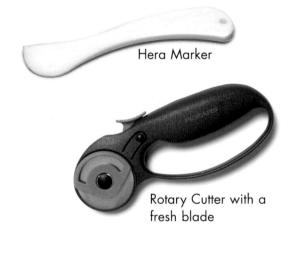

Hera Marker

Rotary Cutter with a
fresh blade

Cutting

Cutting Interfacing

Interfacing is like fabric with a grain because of the way it stretches when sewn. Think of each piece of interfacing as having a top and a bottom. **Cut as if it were directional fabric.**

It's best if your design can be cut from one piece of interfacing. Depending on size of project and interfacing available, you may need to cut several panels of interfacing and place them together to get a large enough piece. Each project diagrams how to cut and place the interfacing based on the stretch. Although it may be more economical to cut differently, cut and place as directed on each pattern.

1. Check the number of squares in your cross stitch pattern across and down. Each pattern lists these measurements.

2. **Cut interfacing to exact sizes** with rotary cutter and 6" x 24" ruler. If you need to cut more than one piece, cut all pieces of interfacing consistently to work with the stretch. Write the word TOP on fusible side with pencil.

3. Trim away partial squares along sides so fusing does not get on iron.

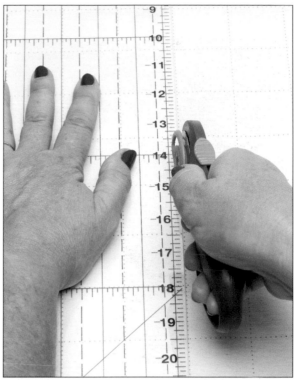

Cut interfacing as if it were directional fabric.

Each project diagrams how to place interfacing based on a grid 15 squares by 16 squares. One panel of QuiltSMART® 1½" fusible interfacing is 15 squares by 16 squares. If the 1½" space between panels is an accurate 1½", you can leave panels together to get the length of pieces you need. If you cut more than one piece, write the word TOP on fusible side of interfacing with pencil.

The 1½" grid printed by HTC Inc. is 32 squares across and sold by the yard. When using this product, refer to two 16 square sections on the diagram.

HTC Inc. is 32 squares wide. For this project you need one width.

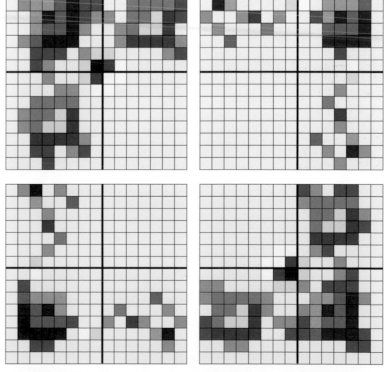

QuiltSMART® is 15 x 16 squares. For this project you need 4 panels.

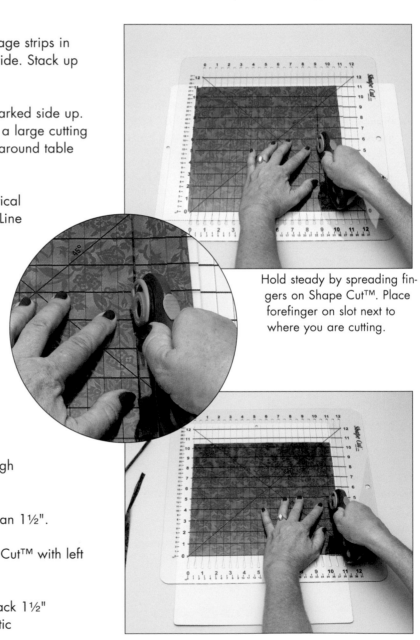

Cutting 1½" Fabric Squares

It's easier to cut up entire pieces of fabric as indicated on yardage charts, and have extra squares than cut and count out specific numbers of squares. They won't be wasted, because you will want to make many of these projects! With the June Tailor Shape Cut, you can cut perfect 1½" squares in a matter of minutes!

June Tailor Shape Cut™ Tool

1. Press fabric. Cut strips into designated widths. Cut strips into fourths at **approximately** 11", or in half at approximately 22".

2. Cut 22" strips in half and 44" selvage to selvage strips in fourths so all pieces are approximately 11" wide. Stack up to four layers right side up.

3. Use 12" x 18" cutting mat with plain, or unmarked side up. Center fabric on cutting mat. If you only have a large cutting mat, cut on the corner of the table, and walk around table for second cut.

4. Place Shape Cut™ on fabric, with slots in vertical position, and two zeros in bottom left corner. Line up horizontal line marked zero with bottom edge of fabric.

5. If edge of fabric needs straightened, place fabric so left edge is slightly to the left of vertical slot marked zero.

6. Square off fabric by placing rotary cutter in vertical slot at zero, and cutting away from you through all layers. Be careful that rotary cutter blade does not cut into side of Shape Cut™.

7. With straight edge of fabric at zero, cut through slots every 1½".

8. Lift Shape Cut™ and remove trimmings less than 1½".

9. Turn cutting mat. Line up zero lines on Shape Cut™ with left and bottom edges of fabric.

10. Cut strips into 1½" squares through slots. Stack 1½" squares by fabric in top of shoe box or plastic embroidery floss box.

Hold steady by spreading fingers on Shape Cut™. Place forefinger on slot next to where you are cutting.

Ruler and Rotary Cutter

1. Press fabric. Cut strips into designated widths. Cut strips into fourths at **approximately** 11", or in half at approximately 22".

2. Cut 22" strips in half and 44" selvage to selvage strips in fourths so all pieces are approximately 11" wide. Stack up to four layers right side up.

3. Use 12" x 18" cutting mat, with grid side up. Center fabric on cutting mat. If you have a large cutting mat, cut on the corner of the table, and walk around table for second cut.

4. If edge of fabric is not already straight, place so left edge of fabric is slightly to the left of vertical line marked zero. Line up horizontal line with bottom edge of fabric.

5. Square off fabric by placing 6" x 12" ruler at zero, and cutting away from you through all layers.

6. With straight edge of fabric at zero, cut strips every 1½". Hold ruler steady by spreading fingers and keeping little finger on fabric.

7. Turn cutting mat. Line up ruler on zero line, and cut.

8. Cut 1½" strips into 1½" squares.

9. Stack 1½" squares by fabric in top of shoe box or plastic embroidery floss box.

General Instructions

Fabric Placement and Fusing Area

1. Check your chart for size of placement area needed. You need an area one third larger than finished size. A 4' x 8' particle board top on sawhorse legs is a perfect surface.

2. Pad surface with bed sheets or cotton batting, and smooth flat. Choose a white sheet so grid lines on the interfacing show through.

3. **Place interfacing on padded surface with textured, fusible side up. Run fingers across interfacing to check for texture.**

4. Butt multiple pieces of interfacing together, lining up grids. **Do not overlap interfacing.**

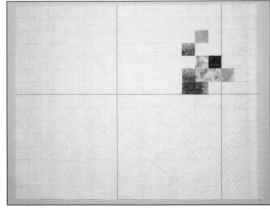

Mark grid into smaller sections on fusible side.

Making Guidelines

1. Mark grid into smaller sections by drawing lines on fusible side with a fine point permanent marking pen, as indicated on charts by black solid lines. An alternative method is to mark grid with pins.

2. (Optional) For quick reference, number interfacing with pencil.

3. Section off areas on chart with self stick 3" note paper so exposed area is area being placed with squares.

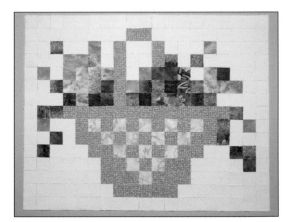

Place 1½" squares on fusible side of interfacing.

Placing and Fusing Squares

1. Place 1½" colored squares right side up and straight on grid with edges of squares touching. Place Background squares last.

2. When every square is in place, carefully steam press with iron on wool setting. Use an up and down pressing motion for 10 seconds or until the squares adhere.

A square can be removed and replaced by pressing the square and quickly peeling it away. However, this should be done sparingly so the interfacing doesn't get damaged.

Carefully press in place with steam iron.

Smaller Fusing Area

If you don't have a surface large enough to lay out the complete pattern at one time, work in smaller units, or one panel at a time.

1. **Place interfacing on table, fusible side up.** Arrange 1½" fabric squares.

2. Place 18" x 24" pressing mat next to interfacing. Holding onto both corners of interfacing, lift and carefully slide interfacing onto pressing mat.

3. Press area with iron, and slide interfacing to next area.

4. After smaller units are pressed, place together on floor area to view complete pattern before stitching.

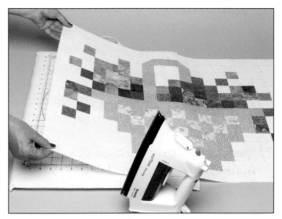

Slide interfacing onto pressing mat.

Making Triangle Pieced Squares

You may wish to give your cross stitch patterns more defined shapes by replacing selected squares with triangle pieced squares made from two different fabrics.

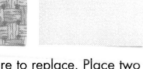

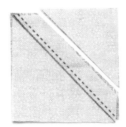
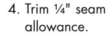

1. Select square to replace. Place two fabrics right sides together.

2. Draw a diagonal line corner to corner.

3. Sew on right side of line.

4. Trim ¼" seam allowance.

5. Set seam, open, and press.

6. Measure. This piece should measure 1½" square.

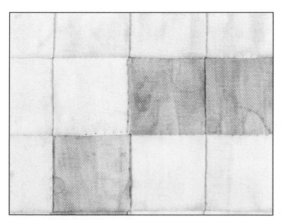

The corner square on this Little Basket was made with a background square.

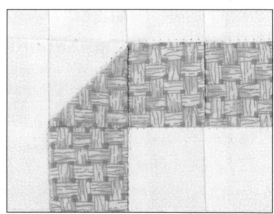

The corner square on this Little Basket was replaced with a triangle pieced square.

Sewing Vertical Rows

1. **Place ¼" foot on sewing machine for accurate piecing.**
Set machine with 15 stitches per inch, or 2.0 setting on computerized machines. If possible, reduce the pressure on your presser foot.

2. Fold far right vertical row right sides together to immediate row on left. Crease edge of row with fingers.

3. Sew vertical row from top to bottom with accurate ¼" seam.

4. Keeping sewn row on top, fold second vertical row to third vertical row, crease, and repeat sewing.

5. **Sew all vertical rows,** always keeping sewn rows on top.

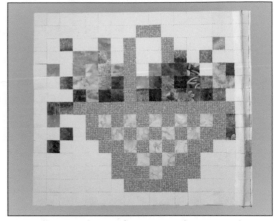

Sew all vertical rows from top to bottom with accurate ¼" seam.

When you have several pieces of interfacing, butt pieces together, and line up grids. Sew all vertical rows before continuing.

Patchwork will shrink to two thirds the original size.

Clipping Vertical Rows

1. Place patchwork with first sewn row in horizontal position.

2. With small, sharp tip scissors, carefully clip lines between squares to stitching.

3. Roll first row up, so second row is in horizontal position. Repeat clipping.

4. Clip all rows, rolling each new row up as you clip.

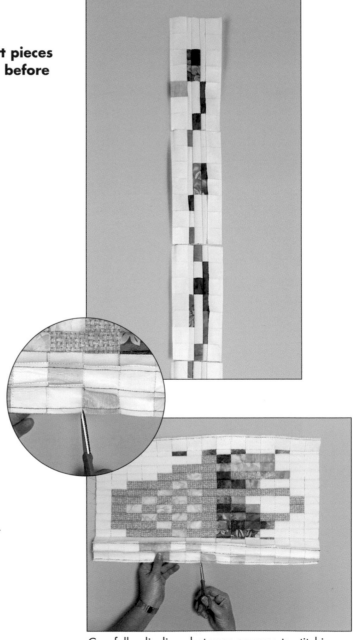

Carefully clip lines between squares to stitching.

Sewing Horizontal Rows

1. Turn patchwork with sewn rows in horizontal position.

2. Fold far right row together to immediate row on left, right sides together. Crease edge of row with fingers.

3. **Finger press the seam allowances in opposite directions. Lock the seams.**

4. Sew row from top to bottom with accurate ¼" seam.

5. Keeping sewn row on top, fold second row to third row, and crease. Following the established pressing pattern, finger press the seam allowances in opposite directions. Lock the seams. Seams should not twist.

6. Sew row from top to bottom.

7. Sew all rows, always keeping sewn rows on top, and finger pressing seams in opposite directions.

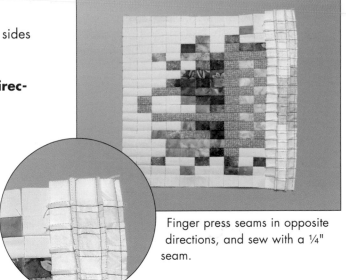

Finger press seams in opposite directions, and sew with a ¼" seam.

Blocking Patchwork

Aggressive pressing distorts the patchwork. Press very carefully.

1. Place patchwork on gridded pressing mat, wrong side up. Line up outside edges of patchwork with lines on pressing mat.

2. Carefully press seams in one direction. Block patchwork with lines on mat as you press.

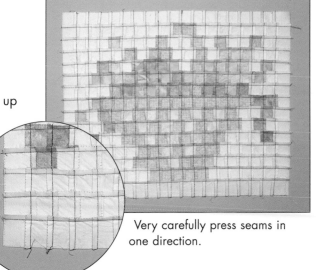

Very carefully press seams in one direction.

3. Turn patchwork right side up. Carefully press from right side.

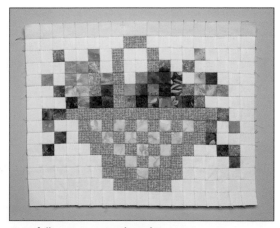

Carefully press on right side.

17

Amber's Basket

Anne Orr wanted her designs to be simple enough for needleworkers, and beautiful Amber's Basket fills the ticket! We've included a working diagram and color insignia chart, just as Anne Orr did.

Teresa Varnes
22" x 25"

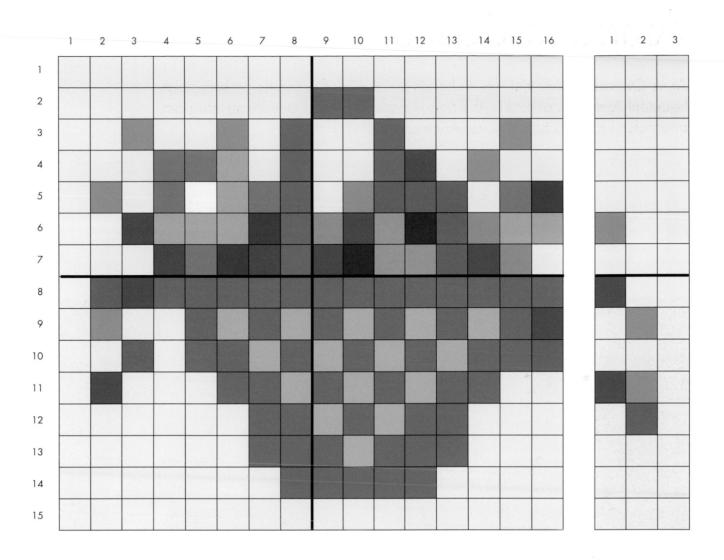

MATERIALS

- **Placement Area**
  22½" x 28½"

- **Fusible Interfacing**
  15 squares x 19 squares
  or 2 QuiltSMART Panels
  or 1 yd plain

- **First Border ⅛ yd**
  (2) 1½" strips

- **Second Border ⅓ yd**
  (3) 3" strips

- **Binding ⅓ yd**
  (3) 3" strips

- **Backing**
  ¾ yd

- **Batting**
  26" x 30"

CUTTING CHART

Color	Yardage	Size Piece to cut	1½" sqs
Background	⅓ yd	12" x 44"	157
Light Pink	⅛ yd	4½" x 11"	3
Medium Pink	⅛ yd	4½" x 11"	9
Dark Pink	⅛ yd	4½" x 11"	2
Light Blue	⅛ yd	4½" x 11"	7
Medium Blue	⅛ yd	4½" x 11"	6
Dark Blue	⅛ yd	4½" x 11"	3
Yellow	⅛ yd	4½" x 11"	1
Light Gold	⅛ yd	4½" x 22"	15
Medium Gold	¼ yd	9" x 22"	57
Medium Green	⅛ yd	4½" x 11"	13
Dark Green	⅛ yd	4½" x 11"	12

Little Basket

The Little Basket Wallhanging is perfect for a child passing away some play hours, or spending time recuperating in bed! Leave the Handle simply squares, or replace the corners with triangle pieced squares.

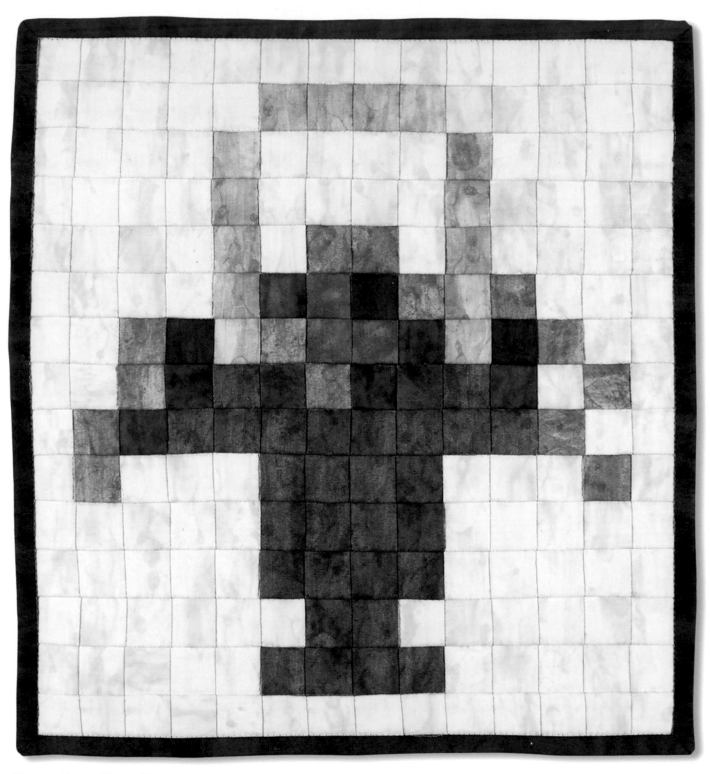

Eleanor Burns, Teresa Varnes
13½" x 14½"

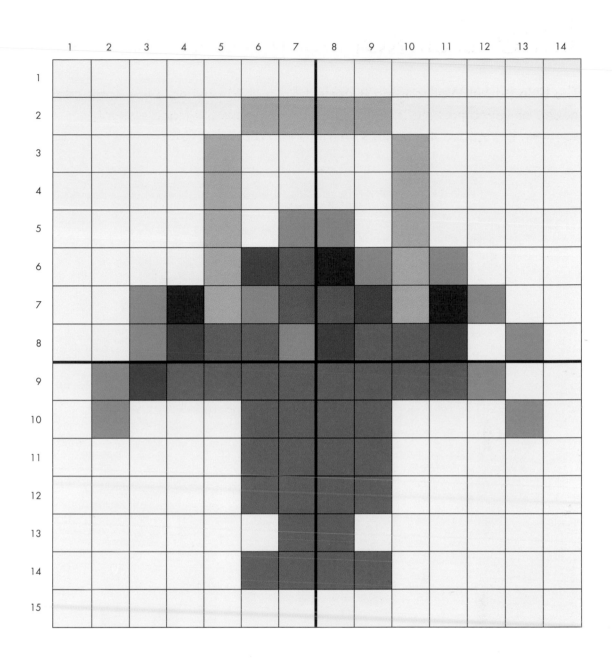

MATERIALS

■ **Placement Area**
21" x 22½"

■ **Fusible Interfacing**
14 squares x 15 squares
or 1 QuiltSMART Panel
or 1 yd plain

■ **Binding ¼ yd**
(2) 3" strips

■ **Backing**
½ yd

■ **Batting**
20" x 20"

CUTTING CHART

Color	Yardage	Size Piece to cut	1½" sqs
Background	¼ yd	9" x 44"	140
Medium Pink	⅛ yd	4½" x 11"	3
Dark Pink	⅛ yd	4½" x 11"	3
Light Gold	⅛ yd	4½" x 11"	14
Medium Gold	⅛ yd	4½" x 44"	30
Medium Green	⅛ yd	4½" x 11"	14
Dark Green	⅛ yd	4½" x 11"	6

Nosegay Wallhanging

Teresa Varnes, Sandy Thompson
33½" x 40"

The hand held, sweet smelling nosegay reached its peak of popularity a century ago, when they were exchanged in lieu of written greetings. This graceful talking bouquet was also known as a tussie mussie.

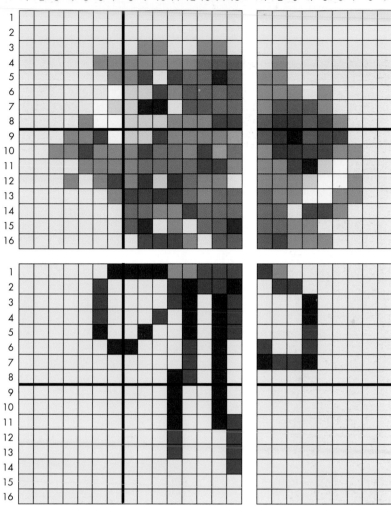

MATERIALS

- **Placement Area**
  36" x 48"

- **Fusible Interfacing**
  24 squares x 32 squares
  or 4 QuiltSMART Panels
  or 3 yds plain

- **First Border** ¼ yd
  (4) 1½" strips

- **Second Border** ⅝ **yd**
  (4) 4½" strips

- **Binding** ⅜ **yd**
  (4) 3" strips

- **Backing**
  1 yd

- **Batting**
  40" x 46"

CUTTING CHART

Color	Yardage	Size Piece to cut	1½" sqs
Background	1 yd	(3) 12" x 44"	513
Light Pink	⅛ yd	4½" x 22"	20
Medium Pink	⅛ yd	4½" x 11"	12
Dark Pink	⅛ yd	4½" x 11"	3
Light Blue	⅛ yd	4½" x 11"	2
Medium Blue	⅛ yd	4½" x 11"	9
Dark Blue	⅛ yd	4½" x 11"	4
Medium Yellow	⅛ yd	4½" x 11"	10
Dark Yellow	⅛ yd	4½" x 11"	12
Light Purple	⅛ yd	4½" x 11"	7
Medium Purple	⅛ yd	4½" x 44"	33
Dark Purple	⅛ yd	4½" x 44"	31
Brown	⅛ yd	4½" x 11"	3
Medium Green	¼ yd	9" x 44"	78
Dark Green	⅛ yd	4½" x 44"	31

Monogram Wallhanging

At one time, fashionable women as Anne Champe Orr carried dainty handkerchiefs embroidered with monograms. This Wallhanging is reminiscent of those elegant days gone by.

Make several photocopies of the chart, and graph the center with your own initials. Repeat a flower in the center, or just leave it blank to show off quilting lines.

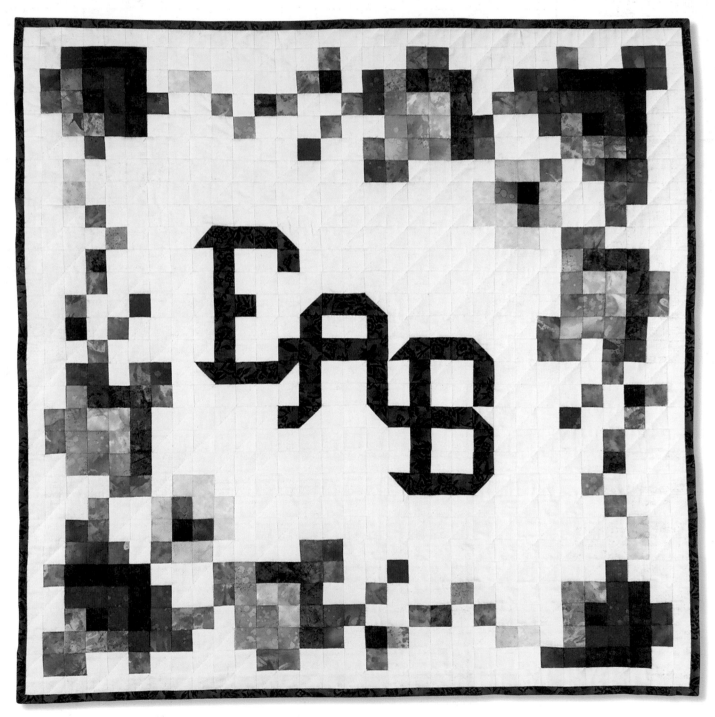

Teresa Varnes
30" x 30"

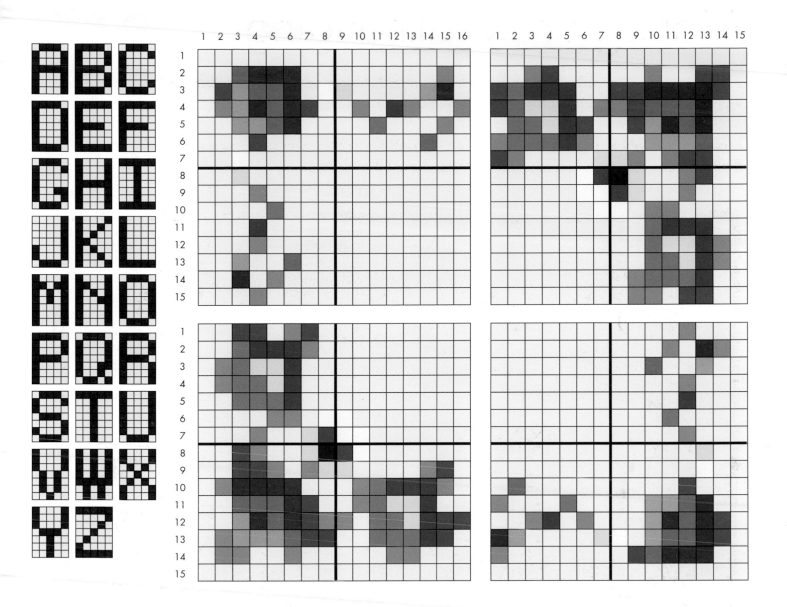

MATERIALS

- **Placement Area**
  45" x 46½"

- **Fusible Interfacing**
  31 squares x 30 squares
  or 4 QuiltSMART Panels
  or 3 yds plain

- **Binding ⅜ yd**
  (4) 3" strips

- **Backing**
  1 yd

- **Batting**
  36" x 36"

CUTTING CHART

Color	Yardage	Size Piece to cut	1½" sqs
Background	1⅓ yd	(4) 12" x 44"	652
Light Pink	⅛ yd	4½" x 22"	20
Medium Pink	⅛ yd	4½" x 22"	24
Dark Pink	⅛ yd	4½" x 44"	32
Medium Blue	⅛ yd	4½" x 44"	32
Dark Blue	⅛ yd	4½" x 22"	28
Medium Yellow	⅛ yd	4½" x 11"	14
Dark Yellow	⅛ yd	4½" x 22"	24
Light Purple	⅛ yd	4½" x 11"	4
Dark Purple	⅛ yd	4½" x 11"	2
Purple Letters	⅛ yd	Based on letter selection	
Medium Green	¼ yd	9" x 22"	60
Dark Green	⅛ yd	4½" x 44"	38

Victorian Basket

The Victorians turned flower giving into an art. Fragrant beauties were used in all ceremonies and rituals of daily life. This easy to make basket of flowers would make a perfect gift for a dear friend.

Eleanor Burns, Teresa Varnes
30" x 30"

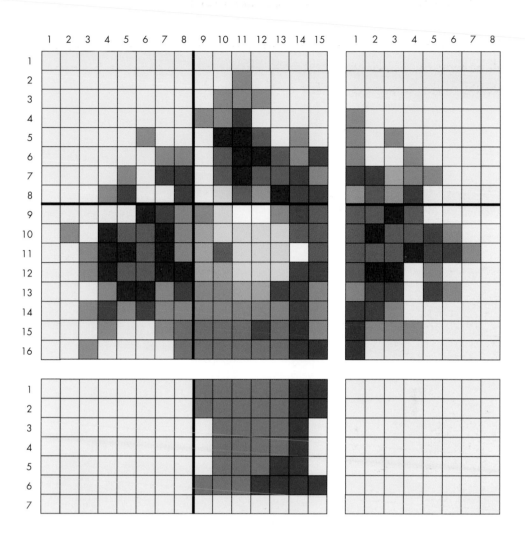

MATERIALS

- **Placement Area**
  34½" x 34½"

- **Fusible Interfacing**
  23 squares x 23 squares
  or 3 QuiltSMART Panels
  or 2 yds plain

- **Folded Border ⅛ yd**
  (2) 1½" strips

- **Border ½ yd**
  (4) 3½" strips

- **Binding ⅜ yd**
  (4) 3" strips

- **Backing**
  1 yd

- **Batting**
  36" x 36"

CUTTING CHART

Color	Yardage	Size Piece to cut	1½" sqs
Background	⅔ yd	(2) 12" x 44"	326
Light Pink	⅛ yd	4½" x 11"	3
Medium Pink	⅛ yd	4½" x 22"	28
Dark Pink	⅛ yd	4½" x 22"	21
Light Yellow	⅛ yd	4½" x 11"	3
Medium Yellow	⅛ yd	4½" x 11"	12
Dark Yellow	⅛ yd	4½" x 11"	7
Medium Blue	⅛ yd	4½" x 22"	25
Dark Blue	⅛ yd	4½" x 22"	17
Medium Green	⅛ yd	4½" x 44"	56
Dark Green	⅛ yd	4½" x 44"	31

Victorian Basket with Border

This Victorian Basket with Border is similar to designs on
fancy boxes of chocolates, or even in needlepoint designs.
It certainly has the feel of Anne Orr's artistic work.

Eleanor Burns, Teresa Varnes
36" x 35"

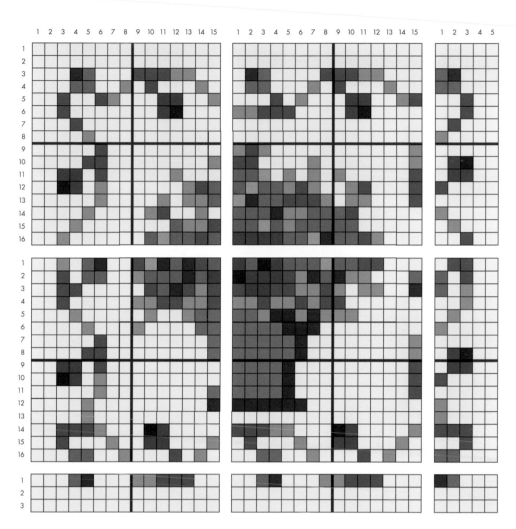

MATERIALS

- **Placement Area**
  52½" x 52½"

- **Fusible Interfacing**
  35 squares x 35 squares
  or 6 QuiltSMART Panels
  or 4 yds plain

- **Binding ⅝ yd**
  (5) 3" strips

- **Backing**
  1¼ yd

- **Batting**
  42" x 42"

CUTTING CHART

Color	Yardage	Size Piece to cut	1½" sqs
Background	1¾ yds	(5) 12" x 44"	831
Light Pink	⅛ yd	4½" x 11"	8
Medium Pink	¼ yd	9" x 22"	64
Dark Pink	⅛ yd	4½" x 22"	17
Light Purple	⅛ yd	4½" x 11"	6
Medium Purple	⅛ yd	4½" x 44"	36
Dark Purple	⅛ yd	4½" x 11"	10
Medium Gold	⅛ yd	4½" x 44"	35
Brown	⅛ yd	4½" x 22"	18
Medium Green	¼ yd	9" x 44"	109
Dark Green	¼ yd	9" x 44"	99

Patty's Basket

Besides making quilt patterns that resembled cross-stitch designs, Anne Orr also designed floral applique quilts. This particular design came from an appliqued quilt named May Baskets featured in a *Better Homes and Gardens* booklet. Patty said she felt like Picasso as she manipulated fabric squares about to create just the right picture.

Patricia Knoechel, Teresa Varnes
35" x 35"

Even though the wall-hanging finishes square, cut interfacing rectangular as directed at 23 squares x 24 squares. Because fusible interfacing stretches going across, the fusible is 23 squares across to compensate for the stretch. The fusible is stable going down, and does not stretch, so it is 24 squares. Both sides should finish the same size.

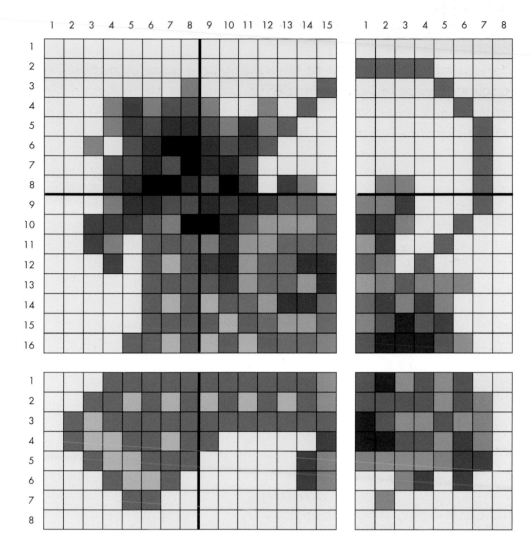

MATERIALS

- **Placement Area**
  34½" x 36"

- **Fusible Interfacing**
  23 squares x 24 squares
  or 4 Quilt SMART® Panels
  or 2 yds plain

- **Folded Border ¼ yd**
  (4) 1¼" strips

- **Border ⅔ yd**
  (4) 5½" strips

- **Binding ⅜ yd**
  (4) 3" strips

- **Backing**
  1⅛ yd

- **Batting**
  40" x 40"

CUTTING CHART

	Color	Yardage	Size Piece to cut	1½" sqs
	Background	⅔ yd	12" x 44"	266
			10" x 20"	
			(2) 10" squares	Corner Triangles
	Light Pink	⅛ yd	4½" x 11"	13
	Medium Pink	⅛ yd	4½" x 22"	16
	Dark Pink	⅛ yd	4½" x 11"	8
	Light Blue	⅛ yd	4½" x 11"	13
	Medium Blue	⅛ yd	4½" x 22"	19
	Dark Blue	⅛ yd	4½" x 11"	8
	Light Purple	⅛ yd	4½" x 11"	13
	Medium Purple	⅛ yd	4½" x 11"	12
	Dark Purple	⅛ yd	4½" x 11"	8
	Light Gold	⅛ yd	4½" x 22"	20
	Medium Gold	¼ yd	9" x 44"	87
	Medium Green	⅛ yd	4½" x 44"	38
	Dark Green	⅛ yd	4½" x 44"	31

Finishing Patty's Basket

1. **Folded Border:** Press 1¼" strips in half lengthwise wrong sides together.

2. Lay folded strip on right side of 5½" Border strip, matching raw edges. Sew ⅛" from raw edges with 10 stitches per inch or 3.0 setting.

3. Cut strips in half.

4. **Corner Triangles:** Draw diagonal lines on two 10" squares. Staystitch ⅛" from both sides of diagonal line. Cut in half on one diagonal.

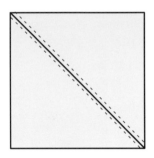

5. Mark dots on wrong side of four triangles ¼" from corners. Measure down 6½" from end of Borders and mark.

6. **First Side:** Flip Triangle to Border and start sewing ¼" from edge of Triangle in order to miter Borders. See dot on Triangle.

7. **Second Side:** Fold first side back out of the way. With second border on top and wrong side up, match 6½" mark to ¼" dot. Sew from ¼" dot to end of triangle.

8. Open strips and press seams toward Triangle. Press Folded Border toward Border.

9. Repeat with remaining three Triangle corners.

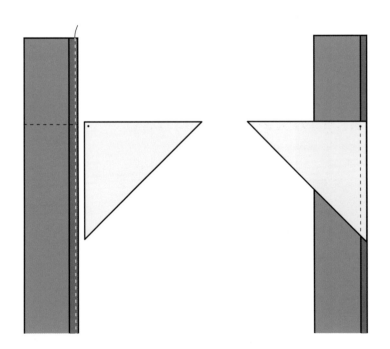

Mitering Corners

1. Place corner on ironing board. Fold top strip under diagonally, and line up strips and Folded Border. Press diagonal crease with iron. Check that corner is square.

2. From wrong side, pin through the lines at the crease, lining up the Folded Border.

3. Sew on diagonal crease, starting at ¼" dot. Trim seam, and press open.

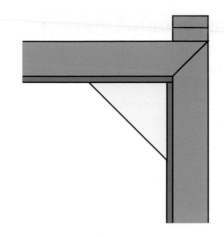

4. Place ruler across edge of Triangle with 45° line on Border's edge. Trim off excess. Repeat with remaining corners.

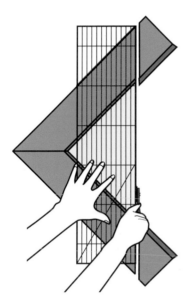

Sewing Triangles to Border

1. Lay out triangles next to quilt top.

2. Finger crease center of each Triangle and match with center of quilt.

3. Pin bias edge to quilt on opposite corners. Sew carefully so bias does not stretch.

4. Fold out. Press seams toward Border. Square off excess with top.

5. Pin and sew on remaining two sides, matching outside edges.

6. Machine quilt and bind.

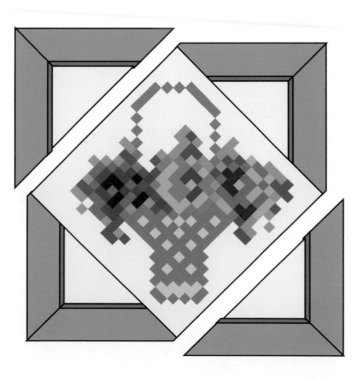

Teresa's Basket

Purchase fabric for this beautiful, nostalgic quilt following the yardage on page 36. Or, if you would like, turn the Pillow Top into a Table runner, or the Basket into a Wallhanging, following each individual yardage chart.

Quilt	85" x 103"
Table Runner	15" x 40"
Wallhanging	40" x 40"

Teresa Varnes, Carol Selepec   85" x 103"

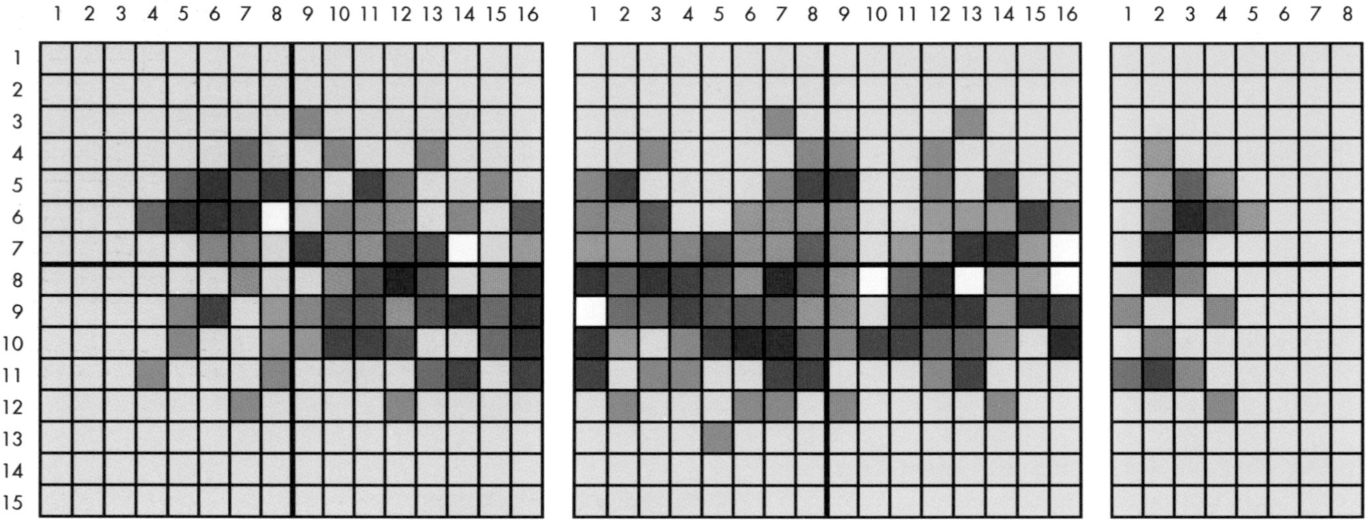

MATERIALS

■ **Placement Area**
60" x 22½"

■ **Fusible Interfacing**
40 squares x 15 squares
or 3 Quilt SMART® Panels
or 2 yds plain

TABLE RUNNER ONLY

■ **Binding ⅓ yd**
(3) 3" strips

■ **Backing**
1¾ yds

■ **Batting**
22" x 46"

CUTTING CHART

Color	Yardage	Size Piece to cut	1½" sqs
Background	⅞ yd	(3) 9" x 44"	413
Light Pink	⅛ yd	4½" x 22"	23
Medium Pink	⅛ yd	4½" x 22"	21
Dark Pink	⅛ yd	4½" x 11"	6
Light Blue	⅛ yd	4½" x 22"	18
Medium Blue	⅛ yd	4½" x 11"	14
Dark Blue	⅛ yd	4½" x 22"	16
Medium Yellow	⅛ yd	4½" x 11"	7
Dark Yellow	⅛ yd	4½" x 11"	6
Medium Green	⅛ yd	4½" x 44"	49
Dark Green	⅛ yd	4½" x 22"	27

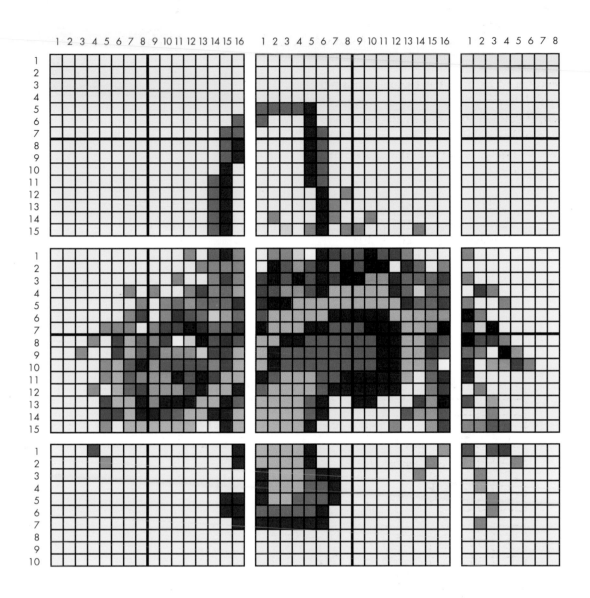

MATERIALS

- **Placement Area**
  60" x 60"

- **Fusible Interfacing**
  40 squares x 40 squares
  or 8 Quilt SMART® Panels
  or 5½ yds plain

WALLHANGING ONLY

- **Binding ⅜ yd**
  (4) 3" strips

- **Backing**
  1¼ yds

- **Batting**
  46" x 46"

CUTTING CHART

Color	Yardage	Size Piece to cut	1½" sqs
Background	2 yds	(6) 12" x 44"	1102
Light Pink	⅛ yd	4½" x 22"	26
Medium Pink	⅛ yd	4½" x 44"	30
Dark Pink	⅛ yd	4½" x 22"	26
Light Blue	⅛ yd	4½" x 11"	5
Medium Blue	⅛ yd	4½" x 22"	22
Dark Blue	⅛ yd	4½" x 11"	13
Medium Yellow	⅛ yd	4½" x 11"	3
Dark Yellow	⅛ yd	4½" x 11"	7
Light Gold	¼ yd	9" x 44"	99
Medium Gold	¼ yd	9" x 44"	71
Brown	¼ yd	9" x 44"	93
Medium Green	¼ yd	9" x 22"	68
Dark Green	⅛ yd	4½" x 44"	35

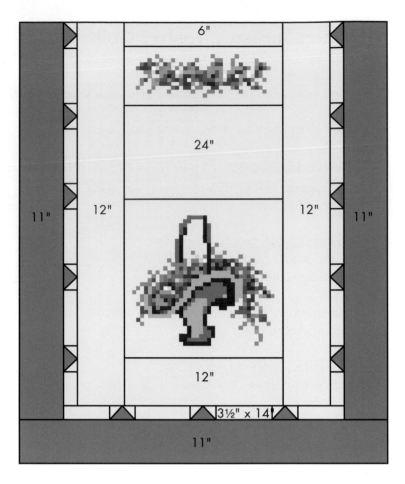

These yardages and measurements are for a queen size quilt, but can be adapted to any bed size simply by changing the width of the Background side panels or Borders.

Refer to the Pillow Cover and Basket on pages 34 and 35 for the amount of interfacing to purchase, plus what size to cut the yardage, and how many 1½" squares to cut.

The border on Anne Orr's quilt was made by appliqueing V shapes on background fabric. We achieved the same look by making flying geese patches and sewing them together with background strips.

COMPLETE QUILT

Basket & Flowers Only			Remainder of the Quilt		
Color	**Yardage**		**Color**	**Yardage**	**Strips to cut**
Light Pink	⅛ yd		Background	6½ yds	(1) 6"
Medium Pink	¼ yd				(1) 24"
Dark Pink	⅛ yd				(5) 12"
Light Blue	⅛ yd				(5) 3½"
Medium Blue	⅛ yd				cut into (14) 3½" x 14"
Dark Blue	⅛ yd		Medium Blue	2½ yds	(7) 11"
Medium Yellow	⅛ yd				
Dark Yellow	⅛ yd		**Flying Geese**		
Light Gold	¼ yd		Background		(3) 3½" strips
Medium Gold	¼ yd				cut into (26) 3½" squares
Brown	¼ yd		Medium Blue		(3) 3½" strips
Medium Green	½ yd				cut into (13) 3½" x 6½"
Dark Green	¼ yd		**Or**		

Flying Geese made with Quilt in a Day's 3" x 6" ruler *

Background		(4) 9" squares
Medium Blue		(4) 7½" squares

*follow instructions included with ruler

Finishing

Binding	1 yd	(10) 3" strips
Backing	8 yds	
Batting	96" x 112"	

Finishing Teresa's Basket Quilt

1. Lay out Basket and Floral Pillow cover with 6", 24", and 12" Background strips.

2. Pin and sew center section together. Trim strips to same length.

3. Piece 12" Background strips, sew to sides, and trim.

Making Thirteen Flying Geese Patches

1. Draw diagonal line on wrong side of (26) 3½" Background squares.

2. Place marked Background squares on (13) 3½" x 6½" Medium rectangles. Sew on drawn lines.

3. Trim seams to ¼". Press seams toward Background.

4. Repeat process with remaining 3½" Background squares.

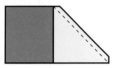

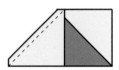
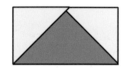

Sewing Geese Borders Together

1. Assembly-line sew (5) Geese patches with (5) 3½" x 14" Background strips.

2. Sew pairs into one strip. Starting at top, pin and sew to Left Border. Trim end.

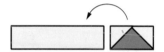

3. Assembly-line sew (8) Geese patches with (8) 3½" x 14" Background strips.

4. Sew five pairs together for Right Border.

5. Starting at top, pin and sew Right Border to mirror Left Border. Trim end.

6. Sew three pairs together for Bottom Border. Sew one 3½" x 14" Background strip to right end.

7. Center, pin, and sew Bottom Border. Trim ends.

8. Piece 11" strips. Pin and sew to Sides, and trim. Press seams toward Medium fabric.

9. Pin and sew to Bottom, and trim.

Floral Wreath

Purchase fabric for this beautiful, nostalgic quilt following the yardage on page 40. Or, if you would like, turn the Pillow Cover into a Table runner, or the Wreath into a Wallhanging, following each individual yardage chart.

Quilt	90" x 102"
Table Runner	15" x 53"
Wallhanging	53" x 53"

Patricia Knoechel, Teresa Varnes, Carol Selepec   90" x 102"

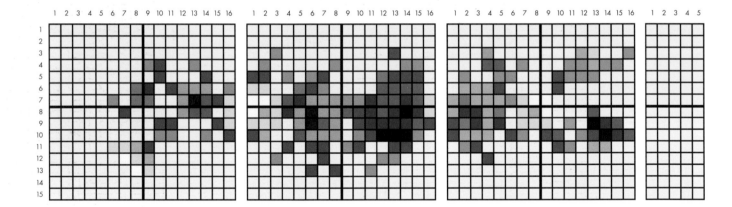

MATERIALS

- **Placement Area**
  79½" x 22½"

- **Fusible Interfacing**
  53 squares x 15 squares
  or 4 Quilt SMART® Panels
  or 2½ yds plain

TABLE RUNNER ONLY

- **Binding ⅜ yd**
  (4) 3" strips

- **Backing**
  1¾ yds

- **Batting**
  22" x 60"

CUTTING CHART

Color	Yardage	Size Piece to cut	1½" sqs
Background	1 yd	(3) 12" x 44"	583
Light Pink	⅛ yd	4½" x 22"	18
Medium Pink	⅛ yd	4½" x 11"	9
Dark Pink	⅛ yd	4½" x 11"	3
Light Blue	⅛ yd	4½" x 11"	14
Medium Blue	⅛ yd	4½" x 11"	8
Dark Blue	⅛ yd	4½" x 11"	5
Light Yellow	⅛ yd	4½" x 11"	8
Medium Yellow	⅛ yd	4½" x 22"	22
Dark Yellow	⅛ yd	4½" x 11"	8
Light Purple	⅛ yd	4½" x 11"	13
Medium Purple	⅛ yd	4½" x 11"	13
Dark Purple	⅛ yd	4½" x 11"	6
Medium Green	⅛ yd	4½" x 44"	41
Dark Green	⅛ yd	4½" x 44"	44

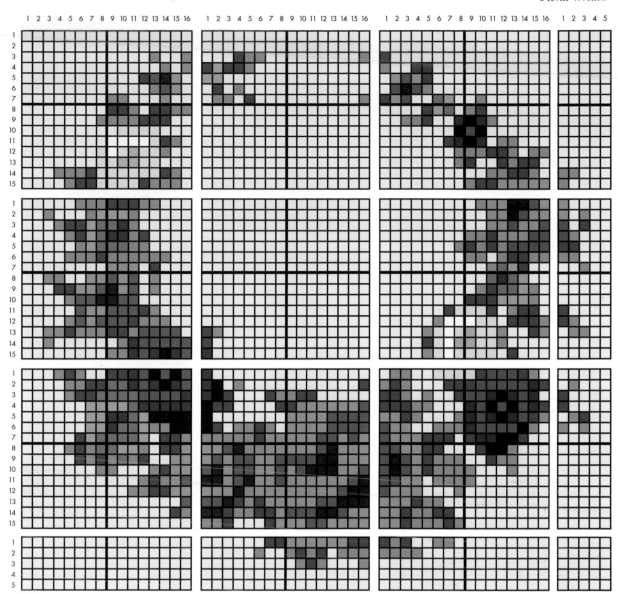

MATERIALS

- **Placement Area**
  79½" x 79½"

- **Fusible Interfacing**
  53 squares x 53 squares
  or 12 Quilt SMART® Panels
  or 8 yds plain

WALLHANGING ONLY

- **Binding ⅝ yd**
  (6) 3" strips

- **Backing**
  3¼ yds

- **Batting**
  60" x 60"

CUTTING CHART

Color	Yardage	Size Piece to cut	1½" sqs
Background	3½ yds	(10) 12" x 44"	1904
Light Pink	⅓ yd	12" x 44"	154
Medium Pink	¼ yd	9" x 44"	88
Dark Pink	⅛ yd	4½" x 44"	33
Light Blue	⅛ yd	4½" x 44"	31
Medium Blue	⅛ yd	4½" x 44"	30
Dark Blue	⅛ yd	4½" x 11"	7
Light Yellow	⅛ yd	4½" x 11"	11
Medium Yellow	⅛ yd	4½" x 44"	44
Dark Yellow	⅛ yd	4½" x 11"	6
Light Purple	⅛ yd	4½" x 44"	41
Medium Purple	⅛ yd	4½" x 44"	34
Dark Purple	⅛ yd	4½" x 22"	28
Medium Green	⅔ yd	(2) 12" x 44"	233
Dark Green	⅓ yd	12" x 44"	165

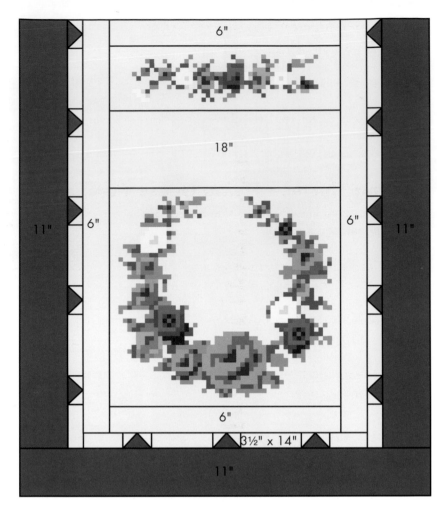

These yardages and measurements are for a queen size quilt, but can be adapted to any bed size simply by changing the width of the Background side panels or Borders.

Refer to the Pillow Cover and Wreath on pages 38 and 39 for the amount of interfacing to purchase, plus what size to cut the yardage, and how many 1½" squares to cut.

The border on Anne Orr's quilt was made by appliqueing V shapes on background fabric. We achieved the same look by making flying geese patches and sewing them together with background strips.

COMPLETE QUILT

Flowers Only			Remainder of the Quilt		
Color	Yardage		Color	Yardage	Strips to cut
Light Pink	⅝ yd		Background	6½ yds	(2) 18"
Medium Pink	¾ yd				(8) 6"
Dark Pink	¼ yd				(5) 3½"
Light Blue	¼ yd				cut into (14) 3½" x 14"
Medium Blue	¼ yd		Medium Purple	2½ yds	(7) 11"
Dark Blue	⅛ yd				
Light Yellow	⅛ yd		**Flying Geese**		
Medium Yellow	¼ yd		Background		(3) 3½" strips
Dark Yellow	⅛ yd				cut into (26) 3½" squares
Light Purple	¼ yd		Medium Purple		(3) 3½" strips
Medium Purple	¼ yd				cut into (13) 3½" x 6½"
Dark Purple	⅛ yd		**Or**		
Medium Green	1 yd		**Flying Geese made with Quilt in a Day's 3" x 6" ruler ***		
Dark Green	¾ yd		Background		(4) 9" squares
			Medium Purple		(4) 7½" squares
			*follow instructions included with ruler		
			Finishing		
			Binding	1 yd	(10) 3" strips
			Backing	9 yds	
			Batting	100" x 112"	

Finishing Floral Wreath Quilt

1. Piece 6" and 18" Background strips.

2. Lay out Wreath and Floral Pillow cover with 6" and 18" Background strips.

3. Pin and sew center section together. Trim strips to same length.

4. Sew 6" Background strips to sides, and trim.

Making Thirteen Flying Geese Patches

1. Draw diagonal line on wrong side of (26) 3½" Background squares.

2. Place marked Background squares on (13) 3½" x 6½" Medium rectangles. Sew on drawn lines.

3. Trim seams to ¼". Press seams toward Background.

4. Repeat process with remaining 3½" Background squares.

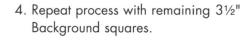
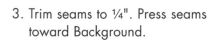

Sewing Geese Borders Together

1. Assembly-line sew (5) Geese patches with (5) 3½" x 14" Background strips.

2. Sew pairs into one strip. Starting at top, pin and sew to Left Border. Trim end.

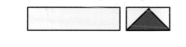

3. Assembly-line sew (8) Geese patches with (8) 3½" x 14" Background strips.

4. Sew five pairs together for Right Border.

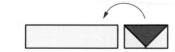

5. Starting at top, pin and sew Right Border to mirror Left Border. Trim end.

6. Sew three pairs together for Bottom Border. Sew one 3½" x 14" Background strip to right end.

7. Center, pin, and sew Bottom Border. Trim ends.

8. Piece 11" Medium strips. Pin and sew to Sides, and trim. Press seams toward Medium fabric.

9. Pin and sew to Bottom, and trim.

Borders

Adding Borders

1. If necessary, square selvage edges on border strips, and piece together.

2. Measure long sides of wallhanging or quilt. Cut two pieces same length from First Border fabric.

3. Pin and sew borders to sides. Set seams, open, and press toward borders. Square corners.

4. Measure top and bottom of quilt from one outside edge to the other, including borders just added.

5. Cut two borders that measurement, pin, and sew. Set seams, open, and press toward borders. Square corners.

6. Repeat steps with remaining borders.

Layering

1. Spread backing right side down without stretching. Clamp or tape fabric.

2. Layer batting on top of backing and pat flat.

3. Center quilt top right side up. Smooth until all layers are flat. Clamp or tape outside edges.

4. Study the quilting on pages 44 and 45, and plan one, or a combination of several. If plans include cross hatch quilting, mark lines with Hera marker.

5. Safety pin layers together every three to five inches next to your quilting lines. Use a pinning tool and 1" safety pins.

Place 6" x 24" ruler on diagonal lines, firmly push Hera marker along edge of ruler, and mark crease for quilting line.

Machine Quilting

Quilting with a Walking Foot

1. Thread machine with thread matching Background, or invisible thread. If using invisible thread, loosen top tension. Match bobbin thread to backing.

2. Attach walking foot, and lengthen stitch to 8 to 10 stitches per inch or 3.5 on computerized machines.

3. Outline flower motifs by spreading seams open, and "stitching in the ditch." Use needle down position to pivot while quilting.

4. "Stitch in the ditch" through straight lines on grid, cross hatching lines, and borders.

5. If you do extensive quilting on the grid, repeat extensive quilting on the borders.

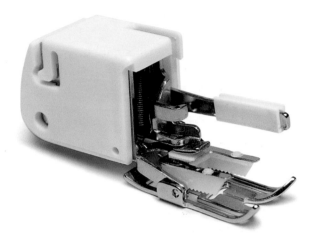

Quilting with a Darning Foot

1. Thread machine with thread matching Background, or invisible thread. If using invisible thread, loosen top tension. Match bobbin thread to backing.

2. Attach darning foot and drop or cover feed dogs with a plate. No stitch length is required as you control the length. Use a fine needle and little hole throat plate with center needle position.

3. Bring bobbin thread up. Lower needle into Background and drop darning foot. Moving fabric very slowly, take a few tiny stitches to lock them. Snip off tails of thread.

4. With your eyes watching ahead, and your fingertips stretching the fabric and acting as a quilting hoop, move fabric in steady motion with machine running at a constant speed.

5. Move fabric underneath needle side to side, and forward and backward. Fill in Background with meandering stitches referred to as stippling, or free-motion stitch around a design.

6. Lock off with tiny stitches and clip threads.

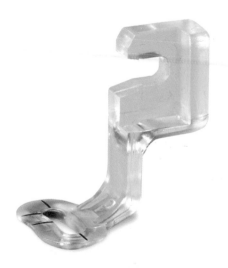

Teresa Varnes

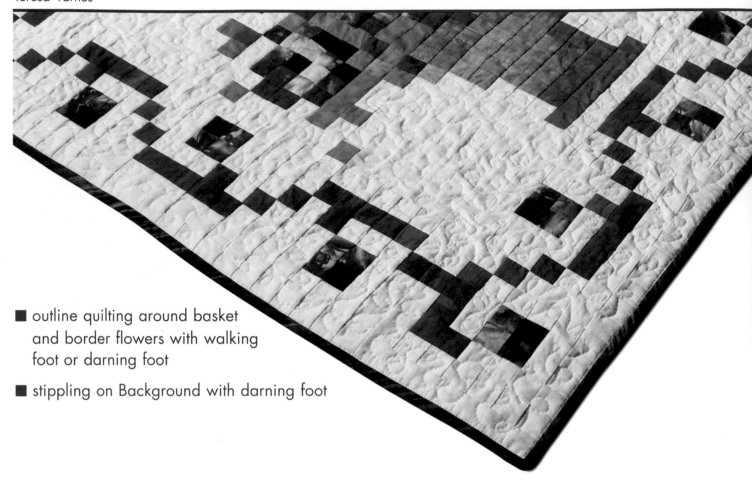

- outline quilting around basket and border flowers with walking foot or darning foot

- stippling on Background with darning foot

Eleanor Burns

- stitch in the ditch on straight grid lines with walking foot

- free motion design with darning foot

- stippling on Borders with darning foot

Sandy Thompson

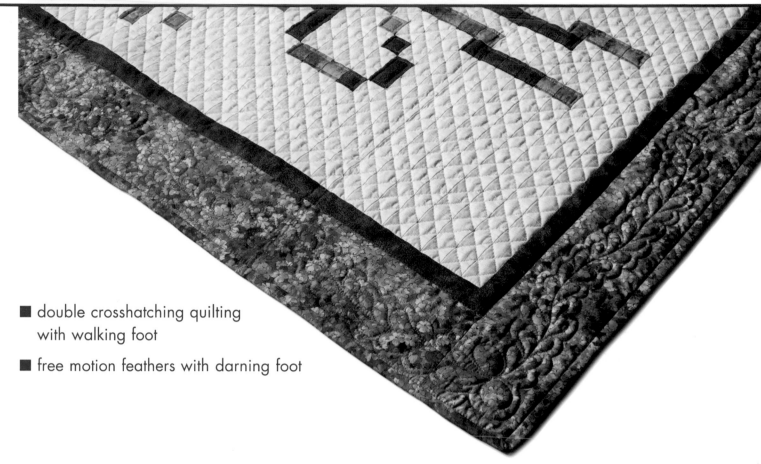

- double crosshatching quilting with walking foot

- free motion feathers with darning foot

Teresa Varnes

- outline quilting around monogram and border flowers with walking foot or darning foot

- crosshatching quilting with walking foot

Binding

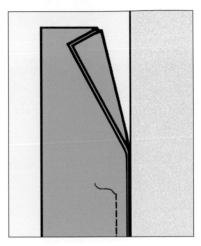

Use a walking foot attachment and regular thread on top and in the bobbin to match the binding.

1. Square off the selvage edges, and sew 3" strips together lengthwise.

2. Fold and press in half with wrong sides together.

3. Line up the raw edges of the folded binding with the raw edges of the quilt in the middle of one side.

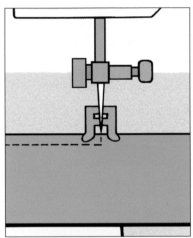

4. Begin stitching 4" from the end of the binding. Sew with 10 stitches per inch, or 3.0 to 3.5.

5. At the corner, stop the stitching ¼" from the edge with the needle in the fabric. Raise the presser foot and turn the quilt to the next side. Put the foot back down.

6. Stitch backwards ¼" to the edge of the binding, raise the foot, and pull the quilt forward slightly.

7. Fold the binding strip straight up on the diagonal. Fingerpress the diagonal fold.

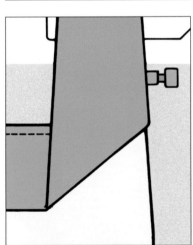

8. Fold the binding strip straight down with the diagonal fold underneath. Line up the top of the fold with the raw edge of the binding underneath.

9. Begin sewing from the edge.

10. Continue stitching and mitering the corners around the outside of the quilt.

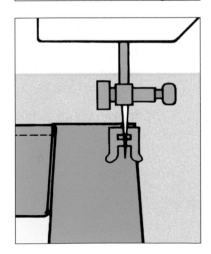

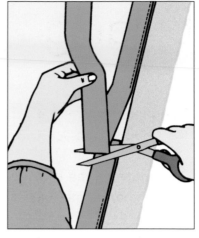

11. Stop stitching 4" from where the ends will overlap.

12. Line up the two ends of binding. Trim the excess with a ½" overlap.

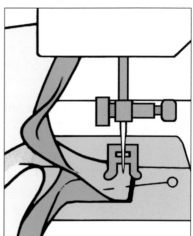

13. Open out the folded ends and pin right sides together. Sew a ¼" seam.

14. Continue to stitch the binding in place.

15. Trim the batting and backing up to the raw edges of the binding.

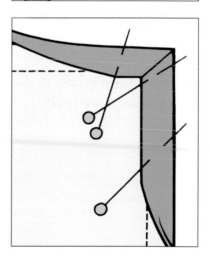

16. Fold the binding to the back side of the quilt. Pin in place so that the folded edge on the binding covers the stitching line. Tuck in the excess fabric at each miter on the diagonal.

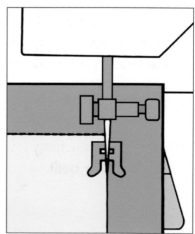

17. From the right side, "stitch in the ditch" using invisible thread on the front side, and a bobbin thread to match the binding on the back side. Catch the folded edge of the binding on the back side with the stitching.
    Optional: Hand stitch binding in place.

Index

Acknowledgments

Grateful thank you to quilters Patricia Knoechel, Carol Selepec, Sandy Thompson, Amber Varnes, Teresa Varnes

Appreciation to suppliers Benartex, Inc, June Tailor, HTC, Inc., Robert Kaufman, QuiltSMART

Order Information

Quilt in a Day books offer a wide range of techniques and are directed toward a variety of skill levels. If you do not have a quilt shop in your area, you may write or call for a complete catalog and current price list of all books and patterns published by Quilt in a Day®, Inc.

Quilt in a Day®, Inc. • 1955 Diamond Street • San Marcos, CA 92069
1 800 777-4852 • Fax: (760) 591-4424 • www.quiltinaday.com